SHE LEADS

SACAGAWEA

Calico Kid
An Imprint of Magic Wagon
abdobooks.com

by **CHRISTINE PLATT**
illustrated by **ADDY RIVERA**

Christine A. Platt is an author and scholar of African and African-American history. A beloved storyteller of the African diaspora, Christine enjoys writing historical fiction and non-fiction for people of all ages. You can learn more about her and her work at christineaplatt.com.

For the Shoshone/Shoshoni Tribe. —CP

To my sister, whose strength and love inspire me. —AR

abdobooks.com

Published by Magic Wagon, a division of ABDO, PO Box 398166, Minneapolis, Minnesota 55439. Copyright © 2020 by Abdo Consulting Group, Inc. International copyrights reserved in all countries. No part of this book may be reproduced in any form without written permission from the publisher. Calico Kid™ is a trademark and logo of Magic Wagon.

Printed in the United States of America, North Mankato, Minnesota.
092019
012020

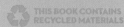
Written by Christine Platt
Illustrated by Addy Rivera
Edited by Bridget O'Brien
Art Directed by Candice Keimig

Library of Congress Control Number: 2019942378

Publisher's Cataloging-in-Publication Data

Names: Platt, Christine, author. | Rivera, Addy, illustrator.
Title: Sacagawea / by Christine Platt ; illustrated by Addy Rivera.
Description: Minneapolis, Minnesota : Magic Wagon, 2020. | Series: Sheroes
Summary: This title introduces readers to Sacagawea and how she became a shero for one of America's most famous expeditions.
Identifiers: ISBN 9781532136443 (lib. bdg.) | ISBN 9781644943106 (pbk.) | ISBN 9781532137044 (ebook) | ISBN 9781532137341 (Read-to-Me ebook)
Subjects: LCSH: Sacagawea--Juvenile literature. | Lewis and Clark Expedition (1804-1806)--Juvenile literature. | Shoshoni women--Biography--Juvenile literature. | Native Americans--North America--Juvenile literature. | Discovery and exploration--Juvenile literature. | Western United States--Juvenile literature
Classification: DDC 978.004974 [B]--dc23

Table of Contents

CHAPTER #1

Girl with a Dream

Around 1788, the Lemhi Shoshone native tribe welcomed their chief's new daughter. Her name was Sacagawea. She would grow up to become a shero for one of America's most famous expeditions.

In the 1700s, information wasn't recorded very well. Few details of Sacagawea's early life are known. Historians are even unsure how to spell her name. Shoshone tribe members say it was likely spelled Sacajawea. It means boat pusher.

The tribe lived in modern-day Idaho. When Sacagawea was about twelve years old, her community was attacked. The Hidatsa tribe captured several girls. She was one of them.

She was taken to modern-day North Dakota. There, she had to work in the fields. She harvested squash and corn.

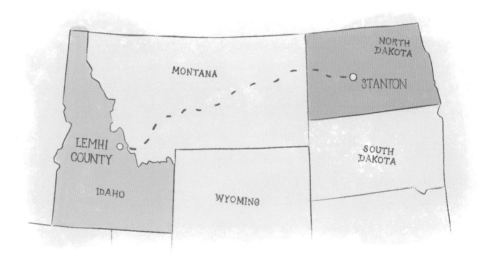

During this time, Europeans were exploring the West. Many of them wanted to settle on native lands. This caused many deadly battles.

But some Europeans gained the trust of native peoples. One was Toussaint Charbonneau. He did not take their land. He lived with them. When he made friends with the Hidatsa, he met Sacagawea.

Some historians say the Hidatsa sold Sacagawea to Toussaint. Others say he won her in a game. Either way, despite her young age, they were married.

Still, Sacagawea never gave up hope. She dreamed of returning to her homeland in the Rocky Mountains.

CHAPTER #2
Woman on a Mission

In 1803, the American government secured land for European settlers. They bought land from the French. This is known as the Louisiana Purchase.

Napoleon Bonaparte was the emperor of France. He sold 828,000 square miles of land to President Thomas Jefferson. This is the largest single land purchase in American history.

The area reached into two Canadian provinces. It also spread across fifteen modern-day states. This included North Dakota where Sacagawea lived.

Many native tribes lived in the area. They believed Napoleon couldn't sell land he didn't own. They fought to save their homelands.

President Jefferson ignored the native people's claim. He believed this was America's newest territory. He formed groups to explore it.

The most famous group was the Lewis and Clark Expedition. It was led by Meriwether Lewis and William Clark. They explored the land from Missouri to the Pacific Coast.

In 1804, the group met a Hidatsa community. This was where Toussaint and Sacagawea lived.

Toussaint spoke French and Hidatsa. Lewis and Clark thought he could be helpful to their trip. They believed Sacagawea would be helpful too. She was familiar with the land.

Sacagawea was expecting her first child. Lewis and Clark expected to meet more tribes. They would be seen as less threatening if a native mother and her child were with them.

Sacagawea feared what might happen if she did not accept their offer. She decided to do whatever she must so they could survive.

She agreed to join them. She would be an interpreter and guide.

CHAPTER #3
So Smart, So Brave

In the winter of 1804, Sacagawea welcomed a son. She named him Jean Baptiste. Lewis and Clark continued their travels in April 1805.

Toussaint and Sacagawea joined them. Jean Baptiste did too. He was tied to his mother's back.

Sacagawea proved to be helpful to Lewis and Clark. She was very smart.

She guided the explorers across difficult land. She taught them about animals they'd never seen before. She also showed them plants and roots that were safe to eat.

Once, Lewis and Clark's boat overturned in a river. Sacagawea saved some of their important documents and travel gear.

Sacagawea honored her name, boat pusher. Lewis and Clark were thankful. They named the river after her.

In the summer of 1805, Sacagawea's dreams finally came true. Lewis and Clark asked for her help. They wanted her to trade with a Shoshone tribe.

Sacagawea went to meet the chief. She discovered it was her brother!

He was so happy to see her. He agreed to the trade. He also offered a guide to help them through the Rocky Mountains.

Sacagawea could not stay with her brother. She had to continue helping Lewis and Clark.

She was happy that her intelligence and bravery helped her survive. They allowed her to see her homeland again.

CHAPTER #4
A Real Shero

In November 1805, Lewis and Clark reached their destination, the Pacific Ocean. Sacagawea wondered at the sandy coast and beautiful blue water.

They camped near the coast for the rest of winter. Then they started on the journey back to Missouri.

The trip took two years, four months, and ten days. Lewis and Clark praised Sacagawea. They might not have made it without her help.

The final years of Sacagawea's life remain a mystery.

Some historians believe she had a daughter named Lizette after the expedition ended. They think she died from fever or illness on December 20, 1812.

Many people hope this was her fate. She wouldn't have seen the forced relocation of native tribes to reservations. This is known as the Trail of Tears.

Others believe she returned to her homeland. There, she would have lived for another seventy years. She would have passed away on April 9, 1884.

If this was her fate, she died before the Shoshone had to leave their homelands. They were moved to the Fort Hall Indian Reservation in 1907.

There is one fact that historians do not debate. Sacagawea was a true shero. She is one of the most famous women in native history.

To learn more about **Sacagawea**, please visit abdobooklinks.com or scan this QR code. These links are routinely monitored and updated to provide the most current information available.